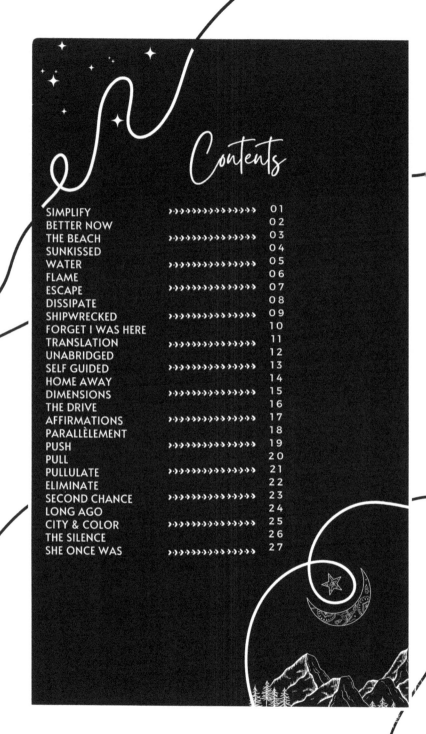

Contents

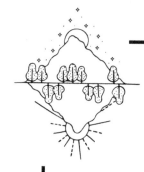

Simplify

See you in my eyes
Profound, tantric, sincere, even
After all these years

So much has since changed
Even the air seems tainted
But then there you are

when I look at you
its like time has seized to move
You've aged in reverse

But you're not seeing
what I do; you're not feeling
Self admiration

you've always been there
Educated. Strong. Complex.
However blinded

Use my eyes to see
Your character underneath
And simplify it

Better Now

I'm sure I've doused
Every bad thought
In gasoline and
Lit my soul
Aflame
But
It
Doesn't
Seem to matter
Either way I still feel
Nothing. An emptiness

Sure
I feel better
I've never felt
So good before
Its like I've
Flipped a
Switch
And
Now
Im
Fine

A sense of inadequacy
somehow more fragile
a heart made of
glass. An
unfused
Soul
So
Yes
I feel
So much
Better now
Thanks for asking

Okay
I fibbed, but
I just had to try
They say if you lie
Enough, you can
Trick yourself
And I've
Tried
Every
Thing
Else

The Beach

I was sand
Emerging from the deep
Salted floors beneath
Only to be washed away
Pushed down and
Under siege
Over and over again
My legs became stagnant castles
Seaweed forming through my veins

You were the ocean
Pulling me in
One step forward
Just to whisk me back again
Under your spell
I stopped fighting
Let you have your way
Holding me down
Pulling me under
I become a part of you
But I lose all of me

Sunkissed

We were golden beautiful
Glowing
We were sunshine
Seeping through silk sheets
Untouched
We were learning
Our bodies
Reading each other's
We were daisies in a field
We were wishes
On a shooting star
Constellations in the sky
We were drifting through
The Northern lights
we were shadows
Dancing on the walls
Light
But dark
Sunkissed
But burnt through

Water

Beneath the cascade rush, she's flying high
Euphoria tumbles like a waterfall's spray
In wild descent, her spirit floats away

With every splash, her troubles wash away
A roaring chorus of enchantment surrounds
Euphoria tumbles like a waterfall's spray

In nature's guild, her heart resounds
Beneath the cascade rush, she's flying high
Euphoria tumbles like a waterfall's spray
Flowing through the motions, she floats away

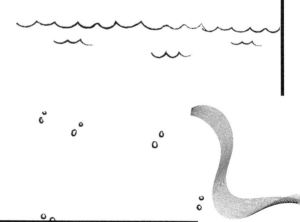

Flame

Amid the flickering flames, anxiety takes root
Like smoldering embers of unease, it feeds her darkest lore
A relentless blaze, a tempest of disquiet
Burning away to unrest

As shadows writhe and restlessness churns even more
The fire's turmoil reflects the storm within her soul
Like smoldering embers of unease, it feeds her darkest lore

The inferno of anxious thoughts, an all-consuming toll
Burning through all hopes of rest
Amid the flickering flames, anxiety takes root
A relentless blaze, a tempest of disquiet
Flames shooting free

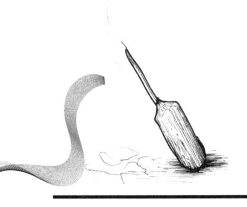

Escape

Nostophobia
In my own space
Frozen in mediocrity

I chose this
Before I knew
What this was

Entrapped in limbo
Nothing hurts
But nothing feels good
Every second that passes
Is a waste of time

I could have left
I could have left
I should have gone

Dissipate

Like dwindling
Silently within

The shadows unseen, then
Neglected and forsaken
My existence transgressing

Anonymity without cause

A silent voice amongst screams
My being dissipates
A phantom within me

And of my own right

Yet somehow calm
Serenity

Shipwrecked

Amidst raging waves
Life's voyage, a shipwrecked dream
Hope's light guides the way

Splintered hull, lost at sea
Winds of change, uncharted territories
Finding strength in the storm

In wreckage, we seek solace
Renewal and peaceful
Find strength in the carnage

Stormy tempest roars
Shipwrecked dreams unfold, hopeful
Renewed redemption ashore

Splintered chassis thrown
Askew, sink their smut below
Enthralled, tenacious

Though through the wreckage
A rebirth in salt and brine
Marooned yet alive,

Forget I was Here

The second
Things get hard
I contemplate
Ways to start over

I'm not good for you here
I'm no use to you here
I'm not kind to myself
But I don't want help

Life should be easy
I didn't choose to start it
I contemplate
Ways to unload it

If I could run
If I could fly
If I could go without
Leaving a trace

You could forget I was here

Translation

In the quiet chambers of my mind
They hide
Intrusive thoughts
Like specters reside
Uninvited
Yet they still invade
Like clusters of mycorhizals
Across a glade
Unwanted pests
That spread like weeds
Ce n'est pas la joie de vivre
L'appel du vide

Vivid as scars
Etched in the mind's design
Unwanted echoes That persist in time
I can't escape
I can't break free
l'heure bleue
Orages la nuit

Still amidst the storm
A moment of constraint
My mind released
Le feu est éteint

Maybe I won't jump today

Unabridged

Don't go
I seem to be
Missing a part of me
I'm trying to make up my mind
Maybe

I'm not
Completely gone
Why can't I ever be
Uncomplicated, unabridged
Wholesome

That's it
Ephemeral
The freeing feeling of
Connecting pieces that are not
Dont go

[Top down, Then bottom up]

Self Guided

Confidently pulling myself
To level with the mountains
Its peaks obscured in the mist of my doubt
A formidable climb, each step uncertain
My ego bruised, heart undaunted
Still I climb

The path meanders, rocky and steep
Challenges hidden around every bend
Waters rushing below in sudden drops
I will press on, I have to
spirit unwavering, unafraid
For in this ascent is all my strength

Each step exerting more and more
My courage tried at every stake
Each stride, a harsh reminder of who I was
Aching to believe I'm unbreakable
I reach for my spirit and set it free
Learning how to let go

Home Away

I found a home in your aura
The hues that complement mine
Our moon phases, completion
A sanctuary of warmth
Home

Deep brown endless eyes
a black hole to somewhere unknown
I found haven in your sweet demeanor
Boundless, selfless

Home

Dimensions

There are untouchable spaces
between the sky the trees
The sun and moon
The Earth the air
Me and you

Dimensions of space
seperating tangibility from concept
on this plane
In this suite
I am me
You are you

The Drive

A winding path
Leads through red woods
Where choices lie ahead
Two paths diverge
Within the light
The Birch trees widespread

The untraveled road
driven only to explore
A trailhead, unleashed
Wonders of world untangled
A vision long pastiche

A soft whisper within
A soft and gentle plea
In the silence of the wood
It speaks
A humbling decree

The drive is long
The path is narrow
Yet the tranquility of mind
Less perilous than the drive itself
This journey I unwind

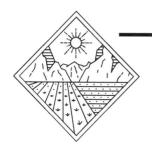

Affirmations

You matter
Your feelings matter
You are capable
You are free
You are kind
You mean well
You are beautiful
You are enough

But me?

I am insignificant
Devoid of real feelings
Am I capable?
I'm tied down
My words hit like daggers
I'm unsettling
I'm unwell
I'm sure it's not enough

It only works if you believe it

Parallèlement

Parallèlement
Deux chemins, à côte à côte
En même temps, la vie

Opposites attract
Magnetic hearts beat forth
Craving connection

We will never be
Nous nous sommes entrelacés
Together... Apart

Push

To break those bounds
And take the leap
It won't be easy

True

But push onward
For throughout the challenges
You discover

The
Real
You

Should you bend
Should you break

Should you dare to lead
Pushing limits
Breaking chains
You find just

What
You
Need

Pull

You've broken bounds
You've tried to leap
You were strong and
You were

Bold

You pushed as hard
As you could handle
You tried to

Break
The
Mold

You may have pulled
You may have fallen

You may have failed to see
Pull yourself through
Do whatever you must
To be who

You
Will
Be

Pullulate

Wispy little
willow leaves
And withering wisteria
Wildly spread across
A field of
Amathyst watsonia
Windy breezes
Tickle the leaves
And gently sends
Them wriggling
Welcoming an autumn gust
A zephyrus withstanding

Water lilies'
White flowerings
Peak just above
The wastelands
Will spread their leaves
So peacefully
On sprouts of fresh wolffia

Want to sink into your field
Of sweet floral wedelia
Wishing we weren't miles away
Justing wishing, hoping, waiting

Eliminate

Will
You still
Be there when
My soul has been
Released, flying limitlessly
Through time and space
Will I still feel you there
holding onto whatever
broad, momentous
deep dark thing
you seem to
see in me
will you
be?

Or
Maybe
you'll think
To yourself what
An absolute relief
as you consider whether
Or not you should have probably
Eliminated me yourself, just to
Cast me out, dismissed me
over some misunderstood
notion only to find that
I had long given up
On everything that
We built together
Because I was
afraid of
losing
you

Second Chance

Thankful for this second chance
Like taking the reigns in my own worthy hands
Because they deserve that much
Instead of settling on the bare minimum
Unexceptional
Senseless
Ennui
Like building something new in the guise of fresh vision
Discovering the profound honor of generational scission
Changing the narrative by trauma elision
Using my words and actions with precision
But I am, thankful for this second chance
To break the cycle
Blessed
Thankful for this second chance
Taking a hold of life, not selling myself short
Deserving more, I'll never just conform,
No longer settling, breaking free from the norm,
Unshackling the chains, a future to transform,
This second chance
I'll take it

Long Ago

Like the little seed sown deep within the soil
Aching, silently aching for sustenance
Where is the light
The water
The life?
Seems like so long ago now
Since we've grown apart

We've adapted to the dark
Where we had buried ourselves
together but far apart
We've gotten so used to dormancy
Striving for comfort
More than trust
More than love
give me roots entwined
intricate connection

So long ago now
Since we've absorbed
Each other's light
Our desires have since dimmed
Content with the mediocracy
Of simply surviving
The ceaseless flow of life,
In the symphony of time

City and Color

I was never cut out for city life
Too much traffic, too much
noise... Too many people in a
hurry; I miss the open ocean
where the sky kisses the sea
Fresh salty breeze drawing
freedom through my hair, hum
hum humming as it combs silently
Untainted air, pure, sweet, clear
Calm and muted hues, paint water
colored skies. Tranquility of slowing
down, To be wholly and truthfully
In the moment without rushing by
You realize that nothing else in the
world matters being except right here
And right now.

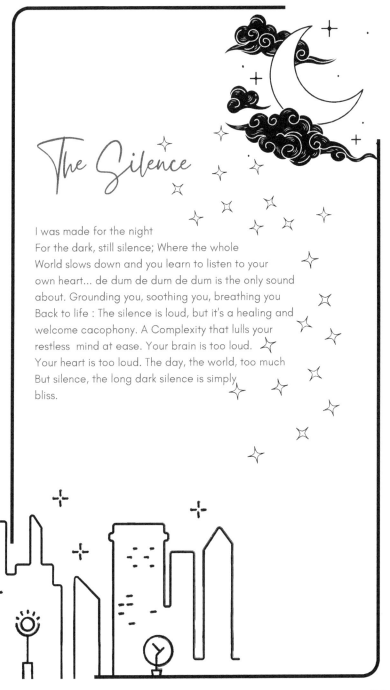

The Silence

I was made for the night
For the dark, still silence; Where the whole
World slows down and you learn to listen to your
own heart... de dum de dum de dum is the only sound
about. Grounding you, soothing you, breathing you
Back to life : The silence is loud, but it's a healing and
welcome cacophony. A Complexity that lulls your
restless mind at ease. Your brain is too loud.
Your heart is too loud. The day, the world, too much
But silence, the long dark silence is simply
bliss.

She Once Was

She once was
The warmth of Mercury rising
A celestial phenomenon
Of embers blazing bright

Radiant
Captivating
Mesmerizing

Resplendent with hope
unbreakable
She was

She Once was
Fervent, untouchable splendor
A luminous aurora
Of silvery prodigy

Moonlit
Alluring
Enchanting

Carefree and airy
Poised
She was

She once was
A goddess of passion
Her essence once danced
A song of wonder and awe

Enticing
Unrelenting
Plentiful

Painting bright golden light
A ballet of beauty
The planets aligned

before her glow was dimmed
She once was

Many many Thanks

To anyone who has ever....

believed in me, supported me, stood by my side. Thank you to everyone who has made my life feel wholesome simply by taking the time to not only listen to my words, but to hear them and consider them. I am deeply humbled by the many many supporters I have, who are willing to experience my work on every level. Thank you to the special few who have never given up on me even when I was hard to handle. And to those who hold space and patience for me to try to understand what my brain is doing. If I had friends as wholesome as you, I would have nothing to write about and I mean that in the best way possible.

There are few things in this world that touch my heart more than being able to touch someone else's.

Thank you for buying my book.

Milton Keynes UK
Ingram Content Group UK Ltd.
UKHW050733201123
432900UK00012B/339